DON'T BE
BY THE S
OF THIS JOURNAL.

Throughout this journal you will find quotes to
inspire you and actions to guide you to get more
out of each day.

You will also find plenty of blank space to capture
your thoughts and ideas about what living more of
your life means to you.

There is no right or wrong way to fill in the blanks
or specific order you need to follow for the actions.

Just close your eyes, breathe deeply and trust
that the page you open will be exactly the one you
need to see.

Used regularly, this journal has the power to
transform your life.

If you want to find out more about living
your happiest and most fulfilling life, visit
domoniquebertolucci.com/life and download
the *Brilliant Life Handbook*.

YOUR TIME IS LIMITED, SO DON'T WASTE IT LIVING SOMEONE ELSE'S LIFE.

STEVE JOBS

TAKE A MINUTE TO THINK ABOUT WHAT MAKES YOU HAPPIEST IN LIFE.

Write down five or six things you know you need in order to be happy and fulfilled.

_____

_____

_____

_____

_____

_____

_____

_____

_____

_____

_____

_____

_____

_____

_____

_____

Think of a big goal or something substantial you would like to achieve. Instead of allowing yourself to become overwhelmed by the size of the task ahead, break it down into small steps and just focus on the first three.

First I will....

_____

_____

_____

Then I will...

_____

_____

_____

After that I will...

_____

_____

_____

* Don't worry about what comes next until you have completed at least the first two items on your list.

—

SIMPLICITY IS THE KEYNOTE OF ALL TRUE ELEGANCE.

COCO CHANEL

—

—

TAKE CARE
OF YOUR BODY.
IT'S THE ONLY
PLACE YOU
HAVE TO LIVE.

JIM ROHN

—

THE KEY TO A LONG AND HEALTHY LIFE IS KNOWING WHEN TO STOP... AND THEN MAKING SURE YOU DO STOP.

If you have a tendency to overindulge, be that with food, alcohol or simply overdoing it, it's time to create new habits.

Make a note of three new habits you can create that will help you take better care of yourself.

1. _____

_____

_____

2. _____

_____

_____

3. _____

_____

_____

YOU DON'T NEED ENDLESS TIME AND PERFECT CONDITIONS. DO IT NOW. DO IT TODAY. DO IT FOR TWENTY MINUTES AND WATCH YOUR HEART START BEATING.

BARBARA SHER

HOW FREQUENTLY YOU SEE YOUR FRIENDS IS NO INDICATOR OF THE QUALITY OF YOUR FRIENDSHIPS. SIMPLY PICK UP WHERE YOU LEFT OFF – WITH TRUE FRIENDS IT WILL FEEL LIKE YOU JUST SPOKE YESTERDAY.

Think of three good friends you haven't been in touch with lately and make a commitment to get back in touch this week.

1. _____

_____

_____

2. _____

_____

_____

3. _____

_____

_____

*So often the people you see the most can be the people whose company you care for the least.

—

HAVE NOTHING IN YOUR HOUSE THAT YOU DO NOT KNOW TO BE USEFUL, OR BELIEVE TO BE BEAUTIFUL.

WILLIAM MORRIS

—

DON'T CONFUSE THE PLEASURE OF LOOKING AT THINGS WITH THE DESIRE TO ACQUIRE THEM.

You don't need to buy something to enjoy a shopping trip. Think of it like visiting a gallery or museum. You can have a lot of fun window shopping and come back home with your money still safe in your wallet.

My five favourite places to go window shopping are:

1. _____

2. _____

3. _____

4. _____

5. _____

—

**THOSE WHO THINK
THEY HAVE NO
TIME FOR
HEALTHY EATING
WILL SOONER
OR LATER HAVE
TO FIND TIME
FOR ILLNESS.**

EDWARD STANLEY

—

YOUR BODY REALLY IS AN AMAZING MACHINE, SO BE MINDFUL OF WHAT YOU FUEL IT WITH.

Make a list of five healthy and nourishing foods you plan to eat more of and five less healthy options you are going to cut back on.

I will eat more...	I will eat less...

**MEN ARE NOT
GREAT OR SMALL
BECAUSE OF
THEIR MATERIAL
POSSESSIONS.
THEY ARE GREAT
OR SMALL
BECAUSE OF WHAT
THEY ARE.**

JAMES CASH PENNEY

IF YOU FIND YOUR BRAIN BUZZING WITH THOUGHTS EVERY WAKING HOUR, AVOID ADDING TO THE CACOPHONY WITH MUSIC, NEWS OR THE LATEST REALITY TV. TURN DEVICES OFF AND ENJOY THE SILENCE.

Think of three times during the day when you plan to switch off whatever is playing and enjoy the silence instead.

I will embrace silence when...

_____

_____

_____

I will embrace silence when...

_____

_____

_____

I will embrace silence when...

_____

_____

_____

—

IT IS NEVER TOO LATE TO BE WHO YOU MIGHT HAVE BEEN.

GEORGE ELIOT

—

THERE'S NO TRUTH IN THE NOTION THAT
YOU ARE TOO OLD TO CHANGE. NO
MATTER HOW BIG OR SMALL THE CHANGE,
THIS IS THE TIME TO MAKE IT HAPPEN.

Write down one change or improvement
you want to make in your life and make the
commitment to do it.

_____

_____

_____

_____

_____

_____

_____

_____

_____

_____

_____

*Regardless of your age, you still have your
whole life ahead of you. Spend it enjoying the new,
improved you.

SAVOUR YOUR MEMORIES. SO OFTEN IT'S THE LITTLE DISCOVERIES THAT YOU MAKE IN THE SPARE MOMENTS OF YOUR LIFE THAT WILL LEAVE THE MOST LASTING IMPRESSION ON YOUR MEMORY.

Think of a small event or something you have witnessed that has become a cherished memory in your life.

—

DON'T CONFUSE HAVING A CAREER WITH HAVING A LIFE.

HILLARY CLINTON

—

THE SECRET OF YOUR FUTURE IS HIDDEN IN YOUR DAILY ROUTINE.

MIKE MURDOCK

HAVING A ROUTINE WON'T MAKE YOU
BORING. IN FACT, NOT HAVING TO THINK
ABOUT DAILY ESSENTIALS WILL MEAN MORE
TIME AND ENERGY TO BE SPONTANEOUS.

Plan your ideal daily routine.

TIME	ACTIVITY

AS SOON AS YOU'RE DONE TRYING TO PLEASE EVERYONE ELSE YOU ACTUALLY HAVE TIME TO MAKE YOURSELF HAPPY.

DELANEY CURRY

EFFICIENCY IS DOING THINGS RIGHT; EFFECTIVENESS IS DOING THE RIGHT THINGS.

PETER DRUCKER

THERE WILL NEVER BE ENOUGH HOURS IN THE DAY TO FINISH EVERYTHING YOU WOULD LIKE TO GET DONE.

Make a note of your three most important priorities today and commit to getting these done before you get started on anything else on your list.

1. _____

_____

_____

2. _____

_____

_____

3. _____

_____

_____

NOTHING IS MORE DEBILITATING THAN LIVING A LIFE OF EXTREMES. TO LIVE A LONG AND HEALTHY LIFE, MAKE SURE YOU TRY A LITTLE BIT OF EVERYTHING AND NOT TOO MUCH OF ANYTHING.

Make a note of three ways you could practise a little more moderation in your life:

**THAT'S WHAT
PEOPLE DO WHO
LOVE YOU.
THEY PUT THEIR
ARMS AROUND
YOU AND LOVE YOU
WHEN YOU'RE NOT
SO LOVABLE.**

DEB CALETTI

—

MY BODY NEEDS LAUGHTER AS MUCH AS IT NEEDS TEARS. BOTH ARE CLEANSERS OF STRESS.

MAHOGANY SILVERRAIN

—

WHEN YOU FEEL OVERWHELMED BY STRESS, DON'T BE BRAVE AND TRY TO SOLDIER THROUGH IT.

Close your eyes, take a few deep breaths and check in with your body. Can you feel any tension in your head, stomach or anywhere else?

Make a note of what you felt in your body and what you plan to do about it, such as go for a walk or talk to a friend.

—

SUCCESS IS NOTHING MORE THAN A FEW SIMPLE DISCIPLINES, PRACTISED EVERY DAY.

JIM ROHN

—

ALWAYS SPEND AS MUCH MONEY AS YOU CAN ON THE BEST QUALITY YOU CAN AFFORD. YOU WILL HAVE FAR FEWER THINGS, BUT THOSE THINGS WILL LOOK AND FEEL GOOD FOR A LONG TIME.

Make a list of the investment items you are saving up for and when you plan to buy them.

ITEM	DATE

THE GROUNDWORK OF ALL HAPPINESS IS HEALTH.

LEIGH HUNT

REPAIR OR REPLACE THINGS THAT ARE BROKEN AS SOON AS POSSIBLE.

It's always annoying to discover something is broken when you go to use it or, even worse, to spend weeks or even months complaining about something that could have been fixed quickly and simply at the time.

I commit to repairing or replacing the following:

- ☐ _____
- ☐ _____
- ☐ _____
- ☐ _____
- ☐ _____
- ☐ _____

—

LIFE IS REALLY SIMPLE, BUT WE INSIST ON MAKING IT COMPLICATED.

CONFUCIUS

—

THERE'S A BIG DIFFERENCE BETWEEN TAKING THE EASY WAY OUT AND LOOKING FOR A SIMPLE SOLUTION. IF YOU ARE FINDING SOMETHING CHALLENGING, TAKE A DEEP BREATH AND ASK YOURSELF, 'HOW CAN I MAKE THIS EASIER?'.

I will find an easier way to...

IF YOU BUY SOMETHING UNSUITABLE, RETURN IT. IF YOU CAN'T, SELL IT, AND IF YOU CAN'T SELL IT, GIVE IT AWAY.

The only thing worse than wasting your money on an erroneous purchase is having it lying around, continually reminding you of your mistake.

I will remove the following from my life:

- _____
- _____
- _____
- _____
- _____
- _____
- _____
- _____
- _____
- _____
- _____
- _____
- _____

ALL YOU NEED
IS LOVE.
BUT A LITTLE
CHOCOLATE
NOW AND THEN
DOESN'T HURT.

CHARLES M. SCHULZ

INDULGENCE (WHETHER IT'S WINE, CHEESE, CHOCOLATE OR ALL THREE) IS HARD TO RESIST – SO REFINE IT INSTEAD.

Rather than overdoing it on cheap-and-cheerful varieties, treat yourself to a small portion of something exceptional. Regardless of your vice, choose the best and savour the experience.

My favourite indulgences are:

- _____
- _____
- _____
- _____
- _____
- _____
- _____
- _____
- _____
- _____
- _____
- _____
- _____

LIFE RUNS IN A NARROW PATH TO BALANCING ACT, CONVINCING TACT, AND SATISFYING FACT.

SANTOSH KALWAR

**THE SECRET
OF HAPPINESS,
YOU SEE,
IS NOT FOUND
IN SEEKING
MORE, BUT IN
DEVELOPING
THE CAPACITY TO
ENJOY LESS.**

SOCRATES

ASK YOURSELF, 'WHAT DO I NEED TO BE HAPPY?' CHANCES ARE NOT ONLY DO YOU NEED VERY LITTLE, BUT YOU ACTUALLY ALREADY HAVE MOST OF IT.

Make a gratitude list of all the things you have in your life that bring you pleasure or joy.

_____

_____

_____

_____

_____

_____

_____

_____

_____

_____

_____

_____

_____

_____

WHEN YOU LIVE A BUSY LIFE, IT'S IMPORTANT TO TAKE TIME OUT TO UNWIND REGULARLY.

Rather than waiting until your stress levels are at their peak, make time each day to sit quietly and relax, regardless of whether or not you feel like you need to.

Today I will recharge by...

_____

_____

_____

_____

_____

_____

_____

_____

_____

_____

_____

_____

—

YOU CAN HAVE IT ALL. YOU JUST CAN'T HAVE IT ALL AT ONCE.

OPRAH WINFREY

—

THERE IS NO SUCH THING AS A FIVE-MINUTE TASK. THE THING YOU THINK WILL TAKE FIVE MINUTES WILL ALWAYS TAKE AT LEAST FIFTEEN. ALWAYS ALLOW MORE TIME THAN YOU NEED AND PLAN TO DO LESS THAN YOU THINK IS POSSIBLE.

Today I will allow extra time for...

YOU CANNOT BE
ALL THINGS TO
ALL PEOPLE.
BE UNIQUE.
BE DIFFERENT.
GIVE TO OTHERS
WHAT YOU WANT
YOURSELF. AND DO
WHAT YOU WERE
MADE TO DO.

ROBERT KIYOSAKI

DON'T TRY TO BE ALL THINGS TO ALL PEOPLE. IT'S OKAY TO SAY 'NO' SOMETIMES. IN FACT, IT'S OKAY TO SAY 'NO' WHENEVER YOU WANT TO.

Today I will say no when...

_____

_____

_____

_____

Today I will say no when...

_____

_____

_____

_____

Today I will say no when...

_____

_____

_____

_____

THE REAL VOYAGE OF DISCOVERY CONSISTS NOT IN SEEKING NEW LANDSCAPES, BUT IN HAVING NEW EYES.

MARCEL PROUST

GIVE THE PEOPLE YOU LOVE THE BEST OF YOU, NOT THE WORST; GIVE THEM YOUR PATIENCE AND RESPECT, AND THE GENEROSITY OF YOUR SPIRIT.

Think of five important people in your life and make note of a compliment you'd like to pay them or kind word you'd like to share with them.

I will tell _____ that I think...

_____

I will tell _____ that I think...

_____

I will tell _____ that I think...

_____

I will tell _____ that I think...

_____

I will tell _____ that I think...

_____

A LITTLE WHILE ALONE IN YOUR ROOM WILL PROVE MORE VALUABLE THAN ANYTHING ELSE THAT COULD EVER BE GIVEN YOU.

RUMI

TAKE THE TIME TO IDENTIFY AND UNDERSTAND YOUR VALUES. YOU DON'T NEED A LOT TO BE HAPPY. YOU JUST NEED TO HAVE THE THINGS THAT MATTER MOST TO YOU.

My core values are:

* Now honour them by integrating them into every part of your life.

IF THE PROBLEM CAN BE SOLVED, WHY WORRY? IF THE PROBLEM CANNOT BE SOLVED, WORRYING WILL DO YOU NO GOOD.

ŚĀNTIDEVA

WORRYING ABOUT SOMETHING WILL NEVER CHANGE ANYTHING. IF THERE IS SOMETHING YOU CAN DO, TAKE ACTION. IF THERE IS NOTHING YOU CAN DO, ACCEPT IT.

Today I will stop worrying about...

_____

_____

and take this action ...

_____

_____

_____

Today I will stop worrying about...

_____

_____

and take this action ...

_____

_____

_____

———

ORGANISE, DON'T AGONISE.

NANCY PELOSI

———

THE ONLY TIME TO BEGIN IS NOW.

If there is something you want to achieve in life, there is no better place to begin than where you are right now. All too often people put off beginning while they wait for some magical sense that 'the time is right'.

Today I will...

_____

_____

_____

_____

_____

_____

_____

_____

_____

_____

_____

_____

_____

_____

MOTIVATION IS WHAT GETS YOU STARTED. HABIT IS WHAT KEEPS YOU GOING.

JIM ROHN

YOU DON'T NEED A LOT OF MOTIVATION TO EXERCISE REGULARLY. ALL YOU NEED IS ENOUGH MOTIVATION TO KEEP YOU GOING UNTIL YOUR NEW HABIT KICKS IN.

Think of a new exercise habit (such as taking a walk at lunchtime) and make a commitment to do it until it becomes natural and easy.

I commit to...

FEELING WELL-DRESSED CAN GIVE YOUR CONFIDENCE A HUGE BOOST, ESPECIALLY IF YOU ARE FEELING UNCOMFORTABLE OR UNCERTAIN.

Think of an outfit or item of clothing that always makes you feel confident and as if you are presenting yourself at your best.

Describe your outfit and how wearing it makes you feel.

_____

_____

_____

_____

_____

_____

_____

_____

*Make a point of tapping into these feelings even when your confidence-boosting clothes are back in the wardrobe.

—

DO NOT WAIT UNTIL THE CONDITIONS ARE PERFECT TO BEGIN. BEGINNING MAKES THE CONDITIONS PERFECT.

ALAN COHEN

—

—

IF YOU ARE NOT CONTENT WITH WHAT YOU HAVE, YOU WOULD NOT BE SATISFIED IF IT WERE DOUBLED.

CHARLES SPURGEON

—

REGARDLESS OF HOW BIG THEIR HOUSES ARE, THE TRUTH IS THAT MOST PEOPLE DO THE MAJORITY OF THEIR LIVING IN ONE SINGLE ROOM.

Describe your favourite room in your home, why you like it and how it makes you feel.

SOMETIMES NOTHING IS THE BEST THING TO SAY AND OFTEN THE BEST THING TO DO.

MICHAEL THOMAS SUNNARBORG

WHILE SHOP DISCOUNTS CAN BE TEMPTING, ASK YOURSELF IF YOU WOULD BE WILLING TO PAY THE FULL PRICE. IF NOT, IT'S NOT A BARGAIN.

Think of three to five discounted things you've bought and make a note of why you would have been better off leaving them on the shelf.

LIFE IS ABOUT BALANCE. THE GOOD AND THE BAD. THE HIGHS AND THE LOWS. THE PIÑA AND THE COLADA.

ELLEN DEGENERES

IN A FULL LIFE, THERE WILL ALWAYS BE UPS AND DOWNS. THE QUALITY OF YOUR LIFE ISN'T DETERMINED BY WHETHER THINGS GO WRONG, BUT HOW QUICKLY YOU DUST YOURSELF OFF WHEN THEY DO.

Think of something in the past that felt like it had 'gone wrong' and make a note of what you learned or how you gained from it.

_____

_____

_____

_____

_____

_____

_____

_____

_____

_____

_____

_____

—

WHAT CAN YOU DO TO PROMOTE WORLD PEACE? GO HOME AND LOVE YOUR FAMILY.

MOTHER TERESA

—

YOU DON'T NEED A LOT OF LUCK TO GET AHEAD IN LIFE, BUT YOU DO NEED TO MAKE AN EFFORT TO MAKE THE MOST OF THE LUCK YOU HAVE.

Think of something in your life that has gone your way unexpectedly or been easier for you than you expected. What was the 'luck' that you were able to make the most of?

*If you put in the groundwork and do the preparation, when a little bit of luck comes along, you will be ready to seize it for all it's worth.

TIME IS WHAT WE WANT MOST, BUT WHAT WE USE WORST.

WILLIAM PENN

TRAVEL MAKES ONE MODEST. YOU SEE WHAT A TINY PLACE YOU OCCUPY IN THE WORLD.

GUSTAVE FLAUBERT

IN ORDER TO UNDERSTAND THE WORLD, ONE HAS TO TURN AWAY FROM IT ON OCCASION.

ALBERT CAMUS

JUST BECAUSE COMMUNICATION HAS BECOME MORE INSTANT, DOESN'T MEAN YOUR RESPONSE ALWAYS HAS TO BE.

Turning your phone on silent or off altogether and reclaiming some silence in your day is important. When are you going to switch off?

I will switch my phone off...

_____

_____

_____

I will turn my phone on silent...

_____

_____

_____

I will have a complete power down...

_____

_____

_____

WHILE THINKING AND PLANNING ARE AN IMPORTANT PART OF ANY PROCESS, THERE IS NO TIME LIKE THE PRESENT TO START DOING WHATEVER IT IS YOU WANT TO DO.

Think of something you want to get done, make a start and see what happens.

Today I will get started by doing...

_____

_____

_____

_____

_____

_____

_____

_____

_____

_____

* There is nothing like action to clarify the mind.

WE SPEND
PRECIOUS HOURS
FEARING THE
INEVITABLE.
IT WOULD BE
WISE TO USE THAT
TIME ADORING
OUR FAMILIES,
CHERISHING OUR
FRIENDS AND LIVING
OUR LIVES.

MAYA ANGELOU

**DON'T LET
YOUR MIND
BULLY YOUR
BODY INTO
BELIEVING IT
MUST CARRY THE
BURDEN OF ITS
WORRIES.**

ASTRID ALAUDA

NOT ONLY IS WORRY EXHAUSTING FOR YOUR MIND, IT ALSO HAS A DEBILITATING EFFECT ON THE BODY.

Instead of letting your mind run in exhaustive circles, start to breathe slowly and evenly. Let the calm return to your mind and the strength return to your body.

Try it and write down how it makes you feel...

_____

_____

_____

_____

_____

_____

_____

_____

_____

_____

NONE OF US KNOWS HOW LONG WE WILL
HAVE IN THIS LIFE, SO MAKE SURE THAT
YOU LIVE EACH DAY OF YOUR LIFE FULLY.

Think of five reasons why today is a good day
to be alive.

Today is a good day to be alive because...

_____

_____

Today is a good day to be alive because...

_____

_____

Today is a good day to be alive because...

_____

_____

Today is a good day to be alive because...

_____

_____

Today is a good day to be alive because...

_____

_____

AMATEURS
SIT AND
WAIT FOR
INSPIRATION,
THE REST
OF US JUST GET
UP AND GO
TO WORK.

STEPHEN KING

IT IS GOOD TO HAVE AN END TO JOURNEY TOWARD; BUT IT IS THE JOURNEY THAT MATTERS, IN THE END.

URSULA K. LE GUIN

REMIND YOURSELF THAT WHAT WILL MATTER AT THE END OF YOUR LIFE ISN'T HOW MANY THINGS YOU HAVE ACHIEVED, BUT HOW MUCH YOU ENJOYED THE RIDE.

Make a note of an experience you've had where even though things didn't turn out as you planned, you still had a really good time.

How did it feel? What did you learn?

_____

_____

_____

_____

_____

_____

_____

_____

_____

_____

_____

—

IT IS BETTER TO BE ALONE THAN IN BAD COMPANY.

GEORGE WASHINGTON

——

THE FIRST
WEALTH IS
HEALTH.

**RALPH WALDO
EMERSON**

—

ALL TRULY GREAT THOUGHTS ARE CONCEIVED WHILE WALKING.

FRIEDRICH NIETZSCHE

—

WHEN YOU ARE FEELING OVERWHELMED
OR CONFUSED ABOUT SOMETHING,
THE BEST THING TO DO IS TO STOP
THINKING ABOUT IT ALTOGETHER.

Go for a walk in the fresh air and allow nature
to clear your mind. Make a commitment to
finding the time to walk this week.

I will walk on...

_____

_____

I will walk for...

_____

_____

I will think about...

_____

_____

I will enjoy my walk because...

_____

_____

—

WE CAN COMPLAIN BECAUSE ROSE BUSHES HAVE THORNS, OR REJOICE BECAUSE THORN BUSHES HAVE ROSES.

ABRAHAM LINCOLN

—

ONE OF THE MOST DESTRUCTIVE WORDS IN THE ENGLISH LANGUAGE IS 'CAN'T'. IT GETS IN THE WAY OF SO MUCH POTENTIAL.

Delete 'can't' from your vocabulary and reframe your past 'can'ts' with affirmative statements instead.

I can...

_____

_____

_____

I am...

_____

_____

_____

I will...

_____

_____

_____

**IT IS NOT
HOW MUCH
WE HAVE,
BUT HOW
MUCH WE
ENJOY, THAT
MAKES
HAPPINESS.**

CHARLES SPURGEON

IF YOU FIND YOURSELF PUTTING THINGS ASIDE AND SAVING THEM FOR 'GOOD' – BE THAT HOMEWARES, CLOTHING, JEWELLERY OR ANY OTHER POSSESSIONS – STOP AND ASK YOURSELF, 'WHAT IS STOPPING ME FROM USING THIS TODAY?'.

Make a list of things you've been saving 'for best' and make a commitment to use them as soon as you can.

_____

_____

_____

_____

_____

_____

_____

_____

_____

*Use the things you love all the time and make every day a special day.

YOU DON'T HAVE TO DO EVERYTHING TO GET AHEAD IN LIFE. WHAT YOU DO NEED TO DO IS A GREAT JOB OF THE THINGS YOU DECIDE TO DO.

Make a list of the things you do a great job of...

_____

_____

_____

_____

_____

_____

_____

_____

_____

_____

_____

_____

_____

_____

—

A GOOD LAUGH IS SUNSHINE IN THE HOUSE.

WILLIAM MAKEPEACE THACKERAY

—

TRUE SILENCE
IS THE REST OF
THE MIND,
AND IS TO
THE SPIRIT
WHAT SLEEP IS
TO THE BODY,
NOURISHMENT
AND
REFRESHMENT.

WILLIAM PENN

YOU DON'T NEED TO CHANT 'OM' TO
MEDITATE. SIMPLY BE SILENT WITH YOUR
THOUGHTS, THEN SET THE THOUGHTS FREE.

Set a timer for five minutes, close your eyes and
breathe. Don't do anything except listen to your
breathing. If a thought comes to you, don't try
to push it away, just ignore it and it will go away
when it's ready.

At the end of your five minutes reflect on how it
made you feel.

_____

_____

_____

_____

_____

_____

_____

_____

_____

_____

_____

DON'T GET SO FOCUSED ON YOUR PROCESS OR ORGANISATIONAL SYSTEMS THAT YOU NEVER GET AROUND TO BENEFITTING FROM THEM.

Think of something you've been putting off until you have the time, money or skill to do it perfectly.

Instead of waiting, make a plan to start where you are today...

_____

_____

_____

_____

_____

_____

_____

*Remind yourself that done is better than perfect. Get started and then make little improvements as you go.

—

DOING GOOD CAN BE AS SIMPLE AS LEAVING ONE HUMAN BEING IN BETTER SHAPE THAN YOU FOUND THEM.

ALEXANDRA FRANZEN

—

THE KEY IS IN NOT SPENDING TIME, BUT IN INVESTING IT.

STEPHEN R. COVEY

IT'S A FACT OF LIFE THAT CERTAIN THINGS NEED DOING AGAIN, AGAIN AND AGAIN.

Rather than reinvent the wheel every time something needs doing, spend the time making a list of all your recurring tasks and commitments.

_____

_____

_____

_____

_____

_____

_____

_____

_____

_____

* Now you can save your brainpower for something else while you work your way through checking them off.

As you do something familiar today, challenge yourself to see it through fresh eyes.

Now reflect on what you have observed...

_____

_____

_____

_____

_____

_____

_____

_____

_____

_____

_____

_____

MAKE A POINT OF TRYING NEW THINGS.
TO LIVE A TRULY BALANCED LIFE YOU NEED
TO FILL IT WITH A VARIETY OF EXPERIENCES.

Make a list of new things you've been meaning
to try or experience. Now make a commitment
to do them.

- [ ] _____
- [ ] _____
- [ ] _____
- [ ] _____
- [ ] _____
- [ ] _____
- [ ] _____
- [ ] _____
- [ ] _____

DON'T EVER TELL YOURSELF THAT YOU'RE NOT GOOD ENOUGH. ALL THAT MATTERS IS THAT YOU TAKE THE RAW MATERIAL YOU'VE GOT AND THEN KEEP WORKING AT IT UNTIL YOU GET TO WHERE YOU WANT TO GO.

Make a note of what would be different in your life if you were living it to your fullest potential.

ENJOY THE LITTLE THINGS, FOR ONE DAY YOU MAY LOOK BACK AND REALISE THEY WERE THE BIG THINGS.

ROBERT BRAULT

ABOUT THE AUTHOR

Domonique Bertolucci is the best-selling author of
The Happiness Code: Ten Keys to Being the Best You Can Be
and the closely guarded secret of some of the world's
most successful people.

Passionate about helping people to get the life they want
and love the life they've got, Domonique has a client list that
reads like a who's who of CEOs and business identities, award-
winning entrepreneurs and celebrities. Her workshops and
online courses are attended by people from all walks of life,
from all around the world. Domonique helps her clients define
their personal happiness prescription and then shows them
exactly how to make it their reality.

Since writing her first book, *Your Best Life*, in 2006,
Domonique has become a world-renowned life strategist and
happiness coach. More than ten million people have seen, read
or heard her advice.

Domonique currently lives in London but her reach is truly
global. In addition to her Australian clients, she has coached
people in London, Amsterdam, Paris, New York, Toronto,
Singapore and Hong Kong. Her weekly newsletter,
Love Your Life, has readers in more than 60 countries.

When she is not working, Domonique's favourite ways to spend
her time are with her husband and two children, reading a good
book and keeping up the great Italian tradition of feeding the
people that you love.

Keep in touch with Domonique at:

domoniquebertolucci.com
facebook.com/domoniquebertolucci
instagram.com/domoniquebertolucci

Sign up for Domonique's free life-coaching course at:
domoniquebertolucci.com/life

Other books by Domonique

The Happiness Code: Ten keys to being the best you can be

Love Your Life: 100 ways to start living the life you deserve

100 Days Happier: Daily inspiration for life-long happiness

Less is More: 101 ways to simplify your life

The Kindness Pact: 8 promises to make you feel good about who you are and the life you live

The Daily Promise: 100 ways to feel happy about your life

Other journals in this series

Be Happy Each Day: A journal for lifelong happiness

Business Development Director *Melanie Gray*
Designer *Maeve Bargman*
Production Director *Vincent Smith*
Production Controller *Jessica Otway*

Published in 2018 by **Hardie Grant Books**, an imprint of
Hardie Grant Publishing

Hardie Grant Books *(Melbourne)*
Building 1, 658 Church Street
Richmond, Victoria 3121

Hardie Grant Books *(London)*
52–54 Southwark Street
London SE1 1UN

hardiegrant.com

ISBN 978 1 74379 430 2
Printed in China